How very practical! I know parisl
rate so many of these methods.

CATHERINE UPCHURCH, *D.*

Whether you are a new catechist looking for ideas to help you get started, or a seasoned catechist looking to expand your repertoire, you will find something comfortable and helpful in this resource.

BRIAN SINGER-TOWNS, *author of* ***The Catholic Faith Handbook for Youth*** *and* ***Biblical Literacy Made Easy****, Director of Content Department, Saint Mary's Press*

Sister Kathleen's ability to inspire the catechist and then give them tools for the classroom is brilliant! This book is a must for all new catechists!

MICKIE ABATEMARCO, *national catechetical leader*

Her experience and common sense show throughout this book. Her suggestions for the communication of solid content are always on the mark. Any teacher of the Catholic faith should use this book.

FATHER JOHN C. VIDMAR, O.P., *Associate Professor of History, Providence College, author of* ***Praying with the Dominicans: To Praise, to Bless, to Preach***

Sr. Kathleen's strong faith, educational experience, and deep understanding of human nature stand out on every page. Anyone whose catechist reads and applies these concepts is blessed indeed.

SUZANNE NELSON, *Adult Faith Formation Coordinator, St. Raphael Church, Rockville, Maryland; online facilitator for VLCFF, Dayton University*

Kathleen Glavich incorporates a solid understanding of the catechetical process and teaching tips galore that even the proven catechist will find helpful.

DANIEL S. MULHALL, *catechist and writer*

This work is a gold mine of ideas for catechists of all levels of experience.

LOUISE E. PROCHASKA PH.D., *Professor of Theology and Women's Studies, Notre Dame College, Cleveland, Ohio*

The book will be a welcomed teaching companion for any catechist.

❧ **Melannie Svoboda, SND**, *retreat director, author of* ***The Lord Is My Shepherd***

As a master catechist herself, Sister Kathleen shares a lifetime of insights that catechists, new or experienced, will find not only useful but encouraging and inspiring.

❧ **Sister Mary Brendon Zajac, SND,** *Professor of Pastoral Theology, Saint Mary Seminary and Graduate School of Theology, Wickliffe, Ohio*

Sister Kathleen's book invites catechists to embrace and share their deepest Christian values, recognizing that invitation and conversion are at the heart of catechesis and evangelization.

❧ **Mary Montour, Assistant Director,** *Office of Evangelization and Catechesis, Archdiocese of Cincinnati*

This book is a great means for a new catechist to learn the fundamentals of teaching our faith, and also a means for veteran catechists to review their teaching methods and keep them sharp.

❧ **Robert Frank,** *lay leader of prayer, catechist, St. Paul Catholic Church, Salem, Ohio*

Sister Kathleen's simple, inspiring, and articulate presentation of the six tasks and practical ways to carry them out makes her the best friend of any catechist.

❧ **Jane Marie Reisinger, SND,** *Director of Religious Education, St. Mary of the Falls Parish, Olmsted Falls, Ohio*

This book is a true inspiration and must-read for every catechist.

❧ **Barbara Doering,** *Principal of Notre Dame Elementary School, Chardon, Ohio*

Sister Kathleen's suggestions and thoughts can help us encourage each student to develop a personal relationship with Christ.

❧ **Tom Brownfield,** *Principal, Holy Family School, Parma, Ohio*

The Six Tasks of Catechesis

The Six Tasks *of* Catechesis

Key Principles *and* Practices *for* Forming Faith

Mary Kathleen Glavich, SND

Twenty-Third Publications
1 Montauk Avenue, Suite 200, New London, CT 06320
(860) 437-3012 » (800) 321-0411 » www.23rdpublications.com

ISBN: 978-1-62785-146-6
Library of Congress Catalog Card Number: 2015957202
Printed in the U.S.A.

Contents

Introduction *1*

1 Your Subject, Jesus Christ *3*

2 Task One: Knowledge of God
and Our Catholic Faith *11*

3 Task Two: The Liturgy, Our Worship *25*

4 Task Three: Moral Formation for Holiness . . *37*

5 Task Four: Prayer, Our Lifeline. *47*

6 Task Five: Community, A Union of Love . . *59*

7 Task Six: Mission to the World. *73*

8 Your Aim: A Complete Picture. *81*

Epilogue *87*

INTRODUCTION

Have you heard the fanciful story about the day the risen Jesus first appears in heaven and meets the angel Gabriel? Shocked to see the Savior's wounds, Gabriel inquires, "Will all human beings know how much you suffered for them?" Jesus replies, "Well, the apostles know, and they will tell others. The word will be passed from generation to generation." "But what if people forget?" Gabriel asks. "Do you have a plan B?" "No," says Jesus. "I'm counting on them."

"Them" is us! In particular, you, who have been called to be a catechist entrusted with delivering the Good News: by dying and rising, Jesus, the Son of God, won eternal life for us. The word *catechesis* is derived from the Greek word for "echo" or "resound." We echo the Good News down through the centuries. The author Frederick Buechner expressed our duty beautifully: "God has a fire He is trying to start with us [that] is a fire that the whole world will live to warm its hands at. It is a fire in the dark that will light the whole world home."

The ministry of catechesis comprises six interrelated tasks that reflect the six dimensions of faith. The *General Directory for Catechesis* (GDC) spells them out, and our *National Directory for Catechesis* reiterates them. Here are the six tasks as given in GDC number 85:

- Promoting knowledge of the faith
- Liturgical education
- Moral formation
- Teaching to pray
- Education for community life
- Missionary education

This book explains what each task entails and suggests ideas for carrying it out.

You might regard these tasks as daunting as the twelve labors of Hercules, especially if you are a beginning catechist. Having taught religion in every grade from first to twelfth, with experience in Catholic schools and parish schools of religion, I've learned quite a bit about what works. By sharing in this book what I've gleaned, I hope to bolster your confidence, sharpen your effectiveness, and increase your joy as you accomplish the six tasks.

Long ago, a largely illiterate population learned the faith through art. Frescoes, statues, mosaics, and stained-glass windows depicted religious people and events. An outstanding example is Michelangelo's paintings in the Sistine Chapel, which proclaim the story of salvation from creation to Judgment Day. Planning a year's religion lessons is much like creating an art masterpiece. It requires certain knowledge, skills, techniques, and materials. Whether you are an apprentice at catechesis or a master, may you find this book a helpful companion.

By the way, thank you for saying yes to the call to be a catechist, someone Jesus can count on!

Your Subject, Jesus Christ

Some artists never tire of painting different views of a particular subject. Degas painted dancers, Monet is known for his landscapes, and Audubon's specialty was birds. We catechists too are fascinated by one subject, Jesus Christ. We present him over and over, lesson after lesson, year after year. By teaching children about Jesus, we set them on the path to eternal life. This is our calling and our passion. *The Catechism of the Catholic Church* says it well:

> At the heart of catechesis we find, in essence, a Person, the Person of Jesus of Nazareth, the only Son from the Father...who suffered and died for us and who now, after rising, is living with us forever. To catechize is "to reveal in the Person of Christ the whole of God's eternal design reaching fulfillment in that Person. It is to seek to understand the meaning of Christ's actions and words and of the signs worked by him." Catechesis aims at putting "people...in communion...with Jesus Christ: only he can lead us to the love of the Father in the

Spirit and make us share in the life of the Holy Trinity." (no. 426)

CHRIST-CENTERED SIX TASKS

A Catholic school teacher asked her third graders, "What has a curly tail, runs up trees, and hides nuts?" One boy whispered to a classmate, "I think the answer is a squirrel, but she probably wants us to say Jesus." This anecdote is an exaggeration, but it does illustrate a fundamental truth: we teach Christ. In fact, each task of catechesis is linked to him.

• ***Teaching knowledge of the faith*** means imparting the truths about the God whom Jesus revealed, the story of salvation in which Jesus is promised (Old Testament) and incarnated (New Testament), the history of the church that Jesus founded, and the teachings of Jesus and his church.

• ***Teaching liturgy*** is presenting the seven sacraments, the acts of Jesus today on behalf of his people. Chief among these is the Eucharist, during which the sacrifice of Jesus is re-presented and he unites himself to us and one another in Communion.

• ***Teaching prayer*** is leading children to foster a relationship with Jesus so that he becomes their best friend and their way, truth, and life.

• ***Teaching moral formation*** is encouraging children to live like Jesus and make decisions in the light of his moral teachings.

• ***Teaching community*** is informing children about Christ's church, the family of God they belong to, and showing them how to take an active role in it.

• ***Teaching mission*** means making children aware of Christ's mandate to spread the Good News, motivating them to do so, and providing opportunities for them to fulfill this responsibility.

RELATIONSHIP WITH US

Besides being focused on Jesus, each task is also grounded in human experience. Knowledge of the faith sheds light on our existence. In the liturgy we offer our lives as a sacrifice. Christian morality flows from and improves human values. Prayer is a channel for alleviating human problems. Community is an expression of our being social creatures. And mission is rooted in our drive to share what is of value.

A HOLY PLACE

Studios are special rooms where artists exercise their passion for creating art. The room where you carry out the six tasks, whether it be a school classroom, a living room, or the rectory basement, is special, too. In fact, it is sacred space because you work to deepen your children's relationship with and commitment to Jesus, the Son of God and our Savior. The room where your religion class is held is no ordinary classroom. It is just as holy as the catacombs or St. Peter's Basilica. When Moses approached the burning bush, God directed him to remove his shoes because he stood on holy ground. Noted educator Thomas Groome recommends that, at least once, catechists remove their shoes before entering their classroom to remind themselves that they are venturing into a holy place.

Furthermore, the textbooks you use are special because they deal with God. You might have them blessed at the start of the year and invite your children to pause for a brief prayer each time they open them.

CREATING A HOLY ATMOSPHERE

Artists make certain that their workspace, the appointments in it, and their materials are conducive to producing their best work. Vincent Van Gogh said, "I see more and more that my work goes infinitely better when I am properly fed, and the paints are there, and the studio and all that." You too can aim for optimal success by setting the stage for carrying out the six tasks.

Neatness. A clean, orderly room makes for a tranquil class. Students are better able to concentrate on the aspect of faith you are teaching.

Quiet. As much as possible, the room should be protected from noise.

Religious decor. A bulletin board or a poster with a religious theme conveys the message that this is a religion class.

A prayer table. A table with an open Bible and items such as a crucifix, a rosary, a candle, and religious statues makes the room more church-like.

Music. Soft, reflective music before class or as a background to prayer or quiet work sets a peaceful tone.

Candles and incense. During prayer times, candles and incense are helpful, if fire laws allow. Flameless candles will do.

A reverent demeanor. Catechists reflect their respect and love for Jesus by a calm, deliberate manner; a well-modulated voice; and professional dress and actions.

CHRIST AS EMMANUEL, GOD WITH US

Artists depend on a muse for inspiration. You can take heart that, because you have been commissioned by Jesus and teach in his name, he teaches through you. You can say with painter William Blake, "I myself do nothing. The Holy Spirit accomplishes all through me." *The Catechism of the Catholic Church* states that "it is Christ alone who teaches—anyone else teaches to the extent that he is Christ's spokesman, enabling Christ to teach with his lips" (no. 427).

Before the *Catechism* told me that Jesus was our invisible partner in the classroom, a friend did. I was teaching ninth-grade religion for the first time. The class had a negative attitude toward religion. In particular, one girl named Barbara seemed determined to give me a hard time. She was smart and challenging. She questioned and argued. Have you met Barbaras in your classes? Many of my well-prepared religion classes that year dissolved into disasters. I doubted that I was carrying out any catechetical task, much less six of them.

Eventually, I confided to a colleague that I was frustrated and discouraged. She counseled me that I should depend on the Holy Spirit, the Spirit of Jesus. She explained that even though I felt like a failure, God was working, and something said or done during the lesson would make a difference in someone's life. So I went on in sheer faith. Then one day, while correcting tests, I discovered this note at the end of Barbara's paper:

Sister, you probably won't believe this, but I go to Mass every day. Through you I discovered that a lot was missing in my life.

You won't always be blessed with such affirmation of your efforts. You might have to wait until the next life to realize what God accomplished through you!

Incidentally, Jesus did promise that wherever two or three are gathered in his name, he is in our midst. Even if you have just one student, Jesus is present.

DISCIPLINE

Any creative endeavor requires discipline. Being a catechist is no exception. It takes self-control to show up each week with a good lesson prepared, especially when you don't feel like it because you are tired, stressed, or in pain. Or maybe your students are a teacher's nightmare. Only your conviction that your ministry is important and your dedication to Jesus can compel you to keep on keeping on.

Discipline is also essential on the part of the students, or your efforts to teach the six tasks will be in vain. Besides praying for your children, especially the troublemakers, you can have good classroom discipline in three main ways:

1. Design lessons that are interesting, appealing, varied, and fun. This is hard work. At least two hours of preparation are needed for an hour-long class.

2. Engage the students by activities other than reading their books or listening to you talk. Let them go to the board, play a game, sing, or carry out a project. Also, don't do anything students can do, such as reviewing a lesson or operating equipment.

3. Show your children respect and love. Greet them. Don't speak about their faults to others. Be fair.

Now, with this foundation, let's forge ahead into examining your six tasks. The remaining chapters explain each one and offer suggestions for incorporating it in your lessons. In keeping with the art theme, each task is associated with a color.

For Reflection and Discussion

- How did God call you to become a catechist? Why did you become one?

- What suggestion do you intend to adopt for making your classroom a holy place?

- When have you been aware that Christ was teaching through you?

- What discipline methods have you seen teachers use effectively?

- Look to Jesus, a master teacher, as a mentor. What methods and style for your ministry can you learn from him?

Task One: Knowledge *of* God *and* Our Catholic Faith

The color blue is a fitting symbol for the task of imparting knowledge of the faith. Not only is blue many people's favorite color, but apparently it is God's favorite color too! Our Creator painted the sky blue, and because oceans and lakes reflect it, they too are blue. What can be known about the Catholic faith is as immense as the sky and as deep as the ocean. We can always learn more, although some mysteries we will never fully comprehend any more than Fido will ever understand an algebraic equation.

Blue is a primary color, which means it mixes with others to form new colors. Similarly, knowledge plays an integral role in each of the other tasks. It is fundamental to catechesis because the first step in forming any relationship is knowledge. We don't love someone unless we first know him or her. If our goal is to bring children into a communion with Christ, it follows that we need to introduce them to Jesus and his teachings.

The source of all that Catholics believe, which is God's revelation, is the Deposit of Faith. It encompasses Scripture (both Old and New Testaments) and Tradition, which is the living transmission of truths from the teaching of the apostles and their successors. Our chief doctrines are expressed in our Creeds and formulated by the magisterium of the church. You are responsible for teaching the slice of knowledge allotted to you in your school's curriculum.

AUTHENTIC TEACHING: BEING TRUE BLUE

At one time, some Catholic religion series were weak in content. Students made one collage after another, and they could expect that the answer to most questions would be "love." Then, in 1996, the National Conference of Catholic Bishops initiated a process for evaluating religion series. A committee of three reviewed those that were submitted to determine if their content was sufficient, free from error, and in harmony with the *Catechism of the Catholic Church.* When publishers brought their series in line with the corrections the committee made, their books were labeled as being in conformity with the *Catechism*. In other words, they were approved for use. This process indicates how seriously the bishops take their teaching role. Today, using an approved religion series guarantees that you are teaching the faith as the church teaches it.

The *Catechism of the Catholic Church* is a valuable reference for catechists. When you would like more information about a topic or when a student or parent stumps you with a question concerning the faith, this book will come to your rescue. If you do not have access to a hard copy, you can download the text as a PDF document from www.usccb.org.

As a representative of the church, in your ministry as a catechist you must take care to present its authentic teachings and not personal interpretations. Also, if you have doubts about a teaching of the church, it is not a good idea to convey this to your students. On the other hand, it is important to inform them that the church, guided by the Holy Spirit, grows in her understanding of the faith and human existence, especially in the light of the changing world around her. Arguably the most famous example of this is the church's need to recant her condemnation of Galileo's theory that Earth revolves around the sun.

A HIERARCHY OF TRUTHS

Blue comes in a cluster of lovely shades. Likewise, the truths of our faith are myriad and varied. Items on to-do lists can be rated urgent, important, and less important. Similarly, the truths of our faith are not all equal; there is a hierarchy to them. Some, like the existence of God and the incarnation, are crucial. Common sense dictates that most class time be devoted to key doctrines. Sometimes the school calendar or limited number of catechetical sessions makes it impossible to cover every lesson in the manual. And sometimes class time allows for teaching only a portion of a lesson. In those cases, the material's significance should determine your decisions of what to teach. What a shame if at the end of the year children know all about the devotion to the Divine Mercy, but they don't realize that Jesus is truly present in the Eucharist!

EXPANDING KNOWLEDGE

I recall hearing a joke about some pesky squirrels. When asked how to get rid of them, a pastor replied, "Just confirm them, and they won't come back." Impress on your children that there is always more to learn about the faith. The *Catechism* is a fat book! Moreover, something new can always be discovered in the Bible. One day I read that God closed the door behind Noah. I never noticed that detail before. Besides, as we read and ponder Scripture, the Holy Spirit gives us fresh insights. In addition, there are two thousand years of church history to explore and hundreds of saints to meet. Graduating from the eighth grade or being confirmed shouldn't halt growth in knowledge of the faith any more than it stops growth in knowledge of math or history.

Inform your students about Catholic websites such as www.vatican.va, www.catholic.org, and www.zenit.org, which delivers daily e-mails containing the pope's homilies and other news about the worldwide church. Encourage them to attend lectures about the faith, take courses on it, join Bible studies, and read Catholic books, magazines, and newspapers.

Of course, you too ought to be lifelong learners when it comes to the faith. The more you know, the better disciple you will be...and the better catechist.

KNOWLEDGE OF THE BIBLE

"Your words were found, and I ate them, and your words became to me a joy and the delight of my heart" (Jeremiah 15:16). How wonderful if our children were nourished and delighted by the word of God! (Our symbol of blue fails us here because food isn't blue.)

It is imperative that your children understand that the Bible is God's word, divine revelation, inspired by the Holy Spirit, and interpreted by the church. You communicate that the Bible is sacred by holding and reading from it with reverence and by enthroning the Bible on a shelf or table. God intends us to take his words in the Bible personally. Present sacred Scripture as a love letter in which God tells us repeatedly that he loves us. Elicit from your students how people read a love letter—slowly, over and over, reading between the lines, and memorizing it. Then state that this is exactly how we are to read the Bible.

If possible, provide a Bible for each child. St. Mary's Press offers Bibles, including Spanish editions, specifically for primary grade, middle grade, and high school students. In parent newsletters or at meetings, encourage reading the Bible together as a family. Suggest that the children keep their Bibles on their pillows and read a few verses every night.

Children should become familiar with the biblical books, their origin, content, purposes, and writing styles. Moreover, they ought to know how to locate verses and use the Bible for prayer. This is a big order. Here are a few ways to fill it:

- Compare a Scripture citation to a house address: the city (book), street (chapter), and house number (verse).

- For practice in looking up passages, have the students write citations for verses, exchange papers, and locate their classmate's verses. Or draw up a list of questions and Bible citations where the answers are found. Hold a contest to see who will answer them all first.

- Compare the types of biblical books to the forms of writing in a newspaper or the kinds of books in a library.

- Assign art projects and writing projects based on biblical stories: posters, dioramas, poems, interviews, and plays.

- To give more insight into biblical stories, have the students rewrite them from the point of view of a character—for example, Goliath's version of the fight with David, or the Canaanite woman's account of her encounter with Jesus.

- Have the students act out stories in the Bible by using a script, miming the event, or forming a tableau.

- Incorporate art masterpieces, songs, and movies related to Scripture in your lessons.

- Include a Scripture reading in every prayer service.

Encourage your students to memorize Scripture verses. Share these tips:

1. Reflect on the meaning of the verse(s).

2. Write the verse several times.

3. Display the verse where you will see it.

4. Make a jigsaw puzzle out of the words of the verse. Make two copies and race with a friend or family member in putting the puzzle together.

5. Make up motions to do or a tune to sing as you say the verse.

6. Work on memorizing a verse right before you go to bed. It sticks better.

7. Set goals for yourself.

Help your children memorize Scripture in class in these ways:

1. Write a verse on the board. Erase one word or phrase at a time and have the children recite the verse each time. When all the words are erased, the class will be saying the verse by heart.

2. Write verses on strips of paper and cut them in half. Distribute them and direct the students to find the half that matches theirs and then memorize the verse.

3. Have the students throw a ball, beanbag, or stuffed animal to one another. Each child who receives the item must recite a chosen verse or add a word to a verse that is being recited.

MASTERING THE TRUTHS IN THE CREED

The Apostles' Creed, which dates from at least the eighth century, is shared by other Christian denominations. It can be prayed at the Eucharist in place of the Nicene Creed and is the opening prayer of the Rosary. In the Rite of Christian Initiation of Adults (RCIA), either the Apostles' Creed or the Nicene Creed, like a precious treasure, is presented to the elect during the third week of Lent after the first scrutiny.

Your students ought to know the Apostles' Creed by heart and the meaning of its words. To teach the prayer, create a worksheet with lines of the prayer on strips. Have the children cut the strips apart and arrange them in order. Or create a crossword puzzle with clues related to words in the prayer. Pray the Creed at the beginning or end of lessons.

Make the doctrines of the church palatable for your children. Explain them in terms their minds can grasp. In the manner of Jesus, who taught about providence by referring to birds and flowers, and of St. Patrick, who compared the Trinity to a three-leaf clover, employ concrete objects in your presentations. Tell stories to illustrate a point. Use analogies to clarify concepts. For example, the union of humanity and divinity in Jesus can be likened to blue and yellow paint mixed to form green paint. The two original colors become inseparable.

Refer to the children's experiences to capture and hold their attention and make the concepts relevant. For example, a lesson on the words "I believe in God" might begin by asking the children what they think God is like and why, or by having them draw a picture that represents God and then explain it.

Since students have different learning styles, present the truths in multiple ways. For instance, to teach about the communion of saints, speak about it for the aural learners, show pictures and diagrams for the visual learners, have material about it read individually for the verbal and solitary learners, and discuss it in groups for the social learners. For the physical learners, teach a finger play or a song about the communion of saints or have the children construct a model of it.

A MAIN METHOD: READING

Teaching religion by reading the textbook and the Bible is as common and comfortable as blue jeans. Sections are usually read by calling on students to read, by reading yourself, or by having the class read silently. However, the lesson would be more interesting if you vary the reading. Bedazzle the blue jeans!

- Direct the class to read a section out loud together.
- Pre-record a section and play it for the class.
- Go around the class in order, having each child read one sentence.
- Have a student read a few sentences and call on someone to continue. The next student does the same. This keeps the students on their toes.
- Assign any speaking parts to different students.

- Assign one part of a long section to each group or row to read silently and summarize for the class.

- Have the students work with partners. Each child reads half a section silently and then reports the main ideas to the partner.

As a section is read, keep the children's attention by instructing them to underline, circle, number, or star key words and concepts. These markings will also help them review the material.

MORE FASCINATING METHODS

Teach in ways that are fun for the children. Play games, show videos, and invite guest speakers. Allow the children to work together with partners or in groups. Avoid making the great truths of our faith boring.

Questions. Both Jesus and Socrates knew the value of questioning. Vary the types of questions you ask: easy and difficult, simple recall, and thought-provoking how and why questions. Engage all of the children simultaneously. For example, if the question requires only a yes or no, direct the students that if the answer is yes, they should raise their right hands. Or you might have them stand, give a thumbs up, put their hands on their heads, or place their fists in front of them. You might have everyone answer at once or turn to a partner to answer the question. If a child asks a question that you can't answer, reply, "I don't know, but I'll find out." Sometimes redirect a student's question to the class.

Discussions. Two side benefits of discussions are that through them students share their faith, and community is created. In your lessons, incorporate different types of discussions: whole class, small group, fishbowl, panel, question box, and problem solving to name a few.

Demonstrations. Concepts come to life and are better remembered when demonstrated. For example, to illustrate the role of Jesus in salvation history, ask several children to stand next to each other. Appoint one student to represent God the Father in heaven and face this line of children at a distance. Tell the line of children to try to reach heaven by one jump. (Make sure they can't do this!) Then lay down a long runner or carpet connecting them and "God," and let them walk across it to heaven. Explain that Jesus is like a bridge that makes it possible for us to reach heaven.

Students as teachers. For a graduate course, we each had to present a miracle of Jesus. I vividly recall my talk on the multiplication of loaves and fish—and probably my classmates do too because homemade bread was served during the break! One of the most effective ways to learn something is to teach it. Provide opportunities for your students to be teachers. Older children could talk to first communicants about the Eucharist. Your class might present a gospel story to another class. Or within your class, a student or a group might give an oral report on a topic.

VOCABULARY

One child thought that manna was "unleaded" bread. Another identified the gift of the church whereby the pope is without error when speaking on matters of faith or morals as "infidelity" instead of "infallibility." Teaching the faith introduces children to words that are unique to religion and new to them. In addition, some familiar words, like *grace* and *brother,* mean something different in religion. The students could keep a notebook and enter new words and their definitions.

MEMORIZATION

My advisor at a secular university demonstrated to me that he was the product of a Catholic school by rattling off, "A sacrament is an outward sign instituted by Christ to give grace." The *Baltimore Catechism* required memorizing answers to questions. While imparting the faith today involves a great deal more than this, memorization is still important. Quoting St. John Paul II, the *General Directory for Catechesis* states, "The blossoms...of faith and piety do not grow in the desert places of a memoryless catechesis" (no. 154).

Your children might enjoy the challenge of memorizing the books of the Bible and the names of the twelve apostles. Perhaps you were taught *Roy G. Biv* to recall the colors of a rainbow. Mnemonic devices can be helpful in religion classes too. *Ro-Co-Co, Gal-Eph-Phi, Col-Thess-Thess, Tim-Tim-Ti, Phil-Heb* is a jingle to remember the first fourteen epistles in order. Teach acronyms. Devise them yourself, like my sentence to remember the order of Israel's provinces of Galilee, Samaria, and Judea: "God Sent Jesus."

REVIEW ACTIVITIES

It's said that adults must hear something seven times before they remember it. Imagine, then, how often we must repeat things to children! Frequently review the beliefs you are teaching. One way is to ask children at the end of a lesson to state one thing they learned. You might also have each student prepare a quiz on a topic and exchange it with a classmate.

A more intriguing way to review concepts is to play games. For added excitement, you might award a prize to the winner or winning team. Here are a few games that are popular with children:

Around the World (Conductor) One child stands beside another child's desk. Ask a question. The first one to slap the desk answers the question (or the first to answer). If correct, that child moves to the next desk. If incorrect, the other child can answer. If he or she is correct, the two children switch places. If both answer correctly simultaneously, ask another question. If neither child can answer, the first person moves to the next child, and either you or another child provides the correct answer.

Jeopardy Make a grid of five categories with five or six answers per category. Assign points for each answer, depending on its difficulty, and write them on sheets of paper. Cover the answers with the corresponding numbered papers. Form three teams and hand each one a bell. The teams choose a category and a number of points and supply the question for the uncovered answer until they are wrong or stumped. For final Jeopardy, the teams bid their points and then write the question to the final answer. The winning team is the one with most points. Where I was DRE, two teachers created the game using PowerPoint and played a recording of the Jeopardy theme song.

Spelling Bee Teams line up across from each other. Pose a question to the first student. If correct, he or she remains standing and the next question is asked of the other side. If incorrect, the student sits and the question goes to the other side. Continue until one child is left.

Baseball Prepare four sets of questions. Code each set as a single, double, triple, or homerun according to difficulty. Draw a diamond on the board. Form two teams and let the players choose a category of question when it is their turn. An incorrect answer is an out. Three outs retires the side. Appoint a scorekeeper to keep track of each team's runs.

FINAL POINTS

Catechists do not just stamp on minds a list of beliefs. As someone noted, teachers are not stuffing turkeys but teaching eagles to fly! There are two kinds of knowledge: head knowledge and heart knowledge. We can know many facts that really don't affect our lives, such as the fact that the sun is approximately ninety-three million miles away. That's head knowledge. Heart knowledge changes us. Someone observed that there is an eleven-inch drop between the head and the heart, and this drop makes all the difference in the world. Eternity depends on it. As catechists, we definitely want to impart head knowledge about Jesus, but more than that, we want to impart heart knowledge that leads children to commit themselves to him and his way of life.

If your lessons are centered around the person of Christ, they will have a more lasting effect. It's comparatively easy to give up a set of beliefs; it's much more difficult to give up a person. Religion lessons should not resemble science, history, or psychology lessons. Rather, through them your students should come to know Jesus as a friend. He, better than anyone else, fits the definition of a friend: someone who knows all about you and likes you anyway. Present Jesus to your children as someone who can and will help them, who cares when it seems as if no one else does, and who has loved them to death. Once they are attracted to Jesus, they will thirst for more knowledge.

Lastly, be a witness to your students. Relating personal stories enhances your teaching and makes a memorable impact. (But don't overdo it!)

Incorporating these ideas in your classes will make you a blue-ribbon catechist!

For Reflection and Discussion

- What five truths of the Catholic faith do you consider essential?
- How have you learned more about the faith as an adult? What means are available to you today?
- When has God spoken to you personally through Scripture?
- What is your favorite Scripture verse? Scripture story?
- How did a certain teacher deepen your relationship with Jesus?

3

Task Two: The Liturgy, Our Worship

The color red grabs attention. This bold color conveys strength, power, passion, and courage. It is the color of blood, fire, and danger signs. As such, red is a fitting symbol for liturgy, our public worship that unites us to Christ and one another. Liturgy channels his life to us—an action paid for by his blood. Through the power of the saving acts of Jesus, his dying and rising, we are purified from sin and can look forward to eternal life. Liturgy comprises the seven sacraments and the Liturgy of the Hours.

Red, which is also the color of valentines, roses, and wine, stands for love. The liturgy is the result of Christ's love for us, and in celebrating it we most powerfully express our love for God. It's no surprise that a second task of catechists is teaching what the liturgy is and preparing children to participate in it wholeheartedly. In fact, Joseph Paprocki, a prominent religious educator, claims that religion lessons should be more like Mass than class.

THE SEVEN SACRAMENTS

The sacraments are acts of Christ and acts of the church through which we receive grace to live as sons and daughters of God. The acronym BE CHAMPs helps children remember them: baptism, Eucharist, confirmation, holy orders, anointing of the sick, matrimony, and penance.

Sacraments of Initiation

Baptism cleanses us of all sin and fills us with grace, virtues, and the gifts of the Holy Spirit. It makes us children of God, heirs of heaven, temples of the Holy Spirit, and members of the church. This first sacrament gives us the right to the other sacraments. ***Confirmation*** completes and intensifies baptismal grace, strengthening our bond to Christ and the church and imparting more power from the Holy Spirit to witness to the faith. The ***Eucharist*** is the source and summit of our Christian life. During it, the sacrifice of Jesus is re-presented and we offer him and ourselves to the Father. We enter into the mystery of Our Lord's dying and rising. At Mass, we hear God speak to us in Scripture, and we become one with Jesus and his church when we receive him in Communion.

Sacraments of Healing

The sacrament of ***penance***, or reconciliation, repairs the damage our sins have caused to our relationships with God and others. We ask pardon and are forgiven. In time of illness, old age, or surgery, the sacrament of the ***anointing of the sick*** brings strength, peace, and courage and results in forgiveness of sins and sometimes physical healing.

Sacraments of Vocation

Matrimony binds a man and women in a covenant in which they promise to love each other exclusively until death. The sacrament gives them grace to be faithful to each other and to raise children, new members of the church. ***Holy Orders*** provides bishops, priests, and deacons to serve the people of God.

TEACHING THE SACRAMENTS

Often our lifegiving sun is a large, red disk. Point out how in the sacraments Jesus, the Son, continues the lifegiving works he performed in Israel. He touches us today by healing, blessing, and forgiving. Prepare a list of Scripture verses related to the sacraments and have the students look up each one and tell what sacrament matches it.

In the sacraments, sensory things and actions play an integral role. Consequently, sacraments are taught effectively by hands-on experiences:

- ***Baptism:*** Let the students enact the rite. They might bless each other with holy water or merely dip their hands into water.

- ***Confirmation:*** Wind and fire symbolize the Holy Spirit. Use a fan or blow dryer to create wind. Light a candle and discuss the power of fire. Anoint the students' hands or foreheads with oil.

- ***Eucharist:*** Arrange for the children to bake bread. Take them to church to see and hold the various items used at Mass.

- ***Penance:*** Put a drop of food coloring in water to represent sin and how it permeates our life.

- ***Anointing of the Sick:*** Apply oil to the students' hands.

- ***Holy Orders:*** Show photos of ordained men who serve in your parish or diocese. Display a stole, the symbol of priesthood.

- ***Matrimony:*** Show rings and discuss their significance. Bring in items from your wedding if possible.

To familiarize younger children with the symbols and rituals of the sacraments, incorporate these elements into your lessons. For example, use a large white candle, processions, bowing, blessings, incense, and holy water.

The most powerful way to learn about the sacraments is to witness or participate in them. You might arrange to have your children present for a baptism, wedding, or anointing. Provide an opportunity for them to celebrate the sacrament of penance or a special Mass that they help plan and in which they take different roles. By the way, for school Masses, having older students sit with younger ones encourages them all to behave.

For memorable lessons, invite guest speakers to talk about their experiences with the sacraments. A mother might explain why she had her baby baptized. An older student could talk about the importance of the sacrament of reconciliation. A senior citizen might explain why the sacrament of the anointing is meaningful to him or her. A married couple could speak about matrimony. Your parish priest or deacon might tell his vocation story.

Form seven groups and assign each group a sacrament to illustrate in art. They might work together to create a poster, a collage, a mural, or a mobile.

Have the children make a booklet about one or more of the sacraments. This may take the form of a scrapbook or a lapbook. Older students might create a PowerPoint presentation.

THE EUCHARIST

Red is the color of power. At the Eucharist, what occurs is so explosive that the poet Annie Dillard proposed that we should all wear crash helmets! By sharing in this feast, a foretaste of heaven, we receive strength to live as Christians. In Russia the word for "red" means beautiful. The Eucharist is beautiful, for through it, Jesus is with us body and blood, soul and divinity. Someday we will experience the fulfillment of Jesus' promise: "Those who eat my flesh and drink my blood have eternal life, and I will raise them up on the last day" (John 6:54). Now, that's power!

Here are various ways to introduce the study of the Eucharist:

- Ask the students to offer reasons for celebrating the Eucharist. They might consult their parents or others.

- Let the children share memories of the most striking Mass they experienced.

- Give a pretest on the Eucharist. On a worksheet, list statements about the Eucharist and include one or two false ones. Have the students mark the statements as true or false. This activity will not only give you an idea of what needs to be taught, but the sheet will serve as a study aid.

- Briefly review (or present) the story of the Exodus, in which God tells his people to celebrate a special Passover meal in remembrance of his great saving acts.

- Features of a birthday party have a parallel in the Mass. Challenge the children to think of pairs such as these:

Birthday Party	Eucharistic Celebration
Table	Altar
Candles on cake	Candles
Guests: family and friends	The congregation
Food: cake and ice cream	Bread and wine
Gifts	Bread and wine, money
Wish	Intercessions
Song: "Happy Birthday"	Hymns
Ritual of opening gifts	Rituals of processions, sign of peace, etc.

- Have older students prepare a PowerPoint showing how the Eucharist is a theme woven through the life of Jesus, beginning with his being placed in a manger, a feedbox, in Bethlehem, a name meaning "house of bread."

- Help students compare the stories of the manna in the desert, the multiplication of the loaves and fish, and the Last Supper. Make a Venn diagram with the stories as headings and fill in elements that are the same and different.

The following activities familiarize children with the order of the Mass and items used during it.

- Present the progression of the Mass as these four actions: we speak to God, God speaks to us, we give gifts to God, and God gives a gift to us.

- Make or find worksheets that reinforce the names of items associated with Mass. These might contain a crossword puzzle, scrambled names for the students to unscramble, or a word search. For the latter two activities, give the fun exercises more substance by asking the students to define each term.

- Create a Bingo game. Prepare cards that have the names (or pictures) of Mass items in the squares and the letters F, E, A, S, T across the top. On slips of paper, write the definitions of these items along with one of the letters. Provide markers to cover the squares. Draw the slips from a box and read the definitions. When a child has a row or column covered and wins, ask him or her to define each covered item to check the answers.

- To review both the order of the Mass and our actions at different parts, list questions about what we do at Mass from beginning to end. Start with "What do we do when we enter the church?" and "What do we do when we come to the pew?" Have the students perform (not say) the answers.

- Write the parts of the Mass on flashcards and have students arrange them in order. You might make one large class set and a small set for each student.

To deepen children's understanding of the Mass, carry out these activities:

- Prepare the readings for the next Sunday's Mass with the students. Read them, give background information, and then ask the students what God is saying in them. You might have older students write a homily based on the gospel. After the Mass, ask the students to report on the homily given at their church.

- To begin and end lessons, pray prayers from the liturgy, perhaps the Collect (opening prayer) of the day.

- Guide your students in analyzing hymns for what they teach about the Mass.

- Send your children (maybe with their families) on a scavenger hunt in church. Give each a sheet with questions like these:
  Where is the baptismal font?
  What mystery is depicted in the main stained-glass window?
  What kind of stations of the cross do we have?
  Where are the holy oils kept?

SACRAMENTALS

Sacramentals are sacred signs such as blessings, medals, scapulars, rosaries, and holy water that through the prayers of the church prepare us to receive the grace of the sacraments and sanctify various aspects of life. They, along with popular devotions, should be taught to children, but only as means to enhance the liturgy, which is far superior to them.

TEACHING THE CHURCH YEAR

Our church (or liturgical) year revolves around the two great mysteries of the incarnation and redemption. We celebrate the four main seasons of Advent, Christmas, Lent, and Easter. There are also thirty-four weeks of Ordinary Time, so called because the weeks are named by the ordinal numbers. Throughout the year there are red-letter days: feasts of the great mysteries like the Ascension and the Immaculate Conception. (It's a good idea to have the children memorize the holy days of obligation.) In tandem with the liturgical cycle is the sanctoral cycle, the celebration of saints' feast days.

A sand dollar is a good visual for introducing the church year. This skeleton of a sea urchin has a poinsettia on one side, and on the reverse side the star of Bethlehem and an Easter lily. Its four holes are said to represent Christ's nail wounds, and the one hole in the center represents the wound caused by a spear. Inside the sand dollar are five pieces in the shape of a star, which when separated resemble doves (for the Holy Spirit) or angels (who sang at the first Christmas).

Have the students draw a circle diagram of the church year in which each season is the color associated with it. They might also make a chart listing the major feast days.

Celebrate the seasons of the church year with your children. For example, observe Advent by making an Advent wreath, a Jesse tree, or a Mary candle in class. Send home newsletters or flyers suggesting ways that families can celebrate Advent, Christmas, Lent, and Easter.

Organize a parish family night of activities for Advent and for Lent. An Advent family night at my parish began with a prayer service. We enjoyed a potluck supper for which one family provided sugar cookies in the shape of the O-antiphon symbols. Then the families created Advent houses out of shoeboxes. Windows showed the O-antiphon symbols that corresponded with the last seven days of Advent and were covered with papers numbered to match the day. The papers would be removed in a countdown to Christmas. Inside the box was a picture of the nativity to be revealed and displayed on Christmas Day.

Provide your children with booklets that contain daily reflections and activities for Advent and Lent. Twenty-Third Publications (23rdpublications.com) is one company that offers these annually along with adult editions.

Red is the international sign for stop. On Sunday, called the Lord's Day, God wants us to stop and rest. We keep this day holy by celebrating Eucharist. Ask your class to suggest other ways to make Sunday special.

LITURGY OF THE HOURS

You probably know that priests pray from a breviary. This is the Liturgy of the Hours, the Church's official daily prayer, also called the Divine Office or Christian Prayer. Ideally it is prayed at seven times (hours) to sanctify the whole day. The hours are composed of psalms, Scripture readings, petitions, and prayers. They correspond to the daily Masses and their celebration of the liturgical seasons and feast days. Monastic communities pray all of the hours, sometimes beginning at 3:15 AM! Although the Liturgy of the Hours is primarily prayed by priests and consecrated religious, all Christians are encouraged to pray at least Morning Prayer and Evening Prayer.

To introduce this component of the liturgy, invite someone who prays it to explain it. Once your students understand what the Liturgy of the Hours is, pray an hour of the day with them by going to www.divineoffice.org or by making copies of a short hour like Midday Prayer.

By teaching the liturgy well, we persuade students to celebrate it and be filled with its graces. We help form children who passionately love Jesus and others. They will be stronger disciples, aflame with red-hot zeal for Christ.

For Reflection and Discussion

- Some people consider everything God created a sacrament. What would be their reasoning?

- What part of the Mass is most meaningful for you? A prayer? A ritual?

- What was the most memorable celebration of the Eucharist you ever experienced? What made it outstanding?

- What is your favorite season of the church year? Your favorite feast day? Why?

- How does praying the Liturgy of the Hours deepen one's spiritual life?

Task Three: Moral Formation *for* Holiness

White is the obvious color to represent the task of moral formation since it stands for goodness. Heroes wear white clothing and ride white horses. In the Book of Revelation, the saints wear white robes. We prefer bright white paper, pure white snow, and white teeth. Moral formation entails teaching right from wrong, forming consciences, and cultivating virtues in students. Mark Twain observed, "To be good is noble. To teach others to be good is more noble."

By engaging in moral formation, you help students fulfill their chief vocation, which is to be holy, Godlike. Our all-good God possesses all virtues to the nth degree. We have the supreme dignity of being children of God, made in God's image and likeness. It follows, then, that we are to reflect his holiness. In doing so, we become what God intended us to be. By being holy, we are fully alive and give glory to God. This leads to union with God for all eternity.

Christ, God made man, teaches us the way to holiness. He instructed us in the Sermon on the Mount, affirmed the Ten

Commandments, and gave us the Beatitudes. He identified love of God as the greatest commandment, and love of neighbor as the second greatest. He gave us a new commandment to love one another as he loves us. Jesus also taught right living by his actions. He humbled himself to become man, submitted to the Father's will, associated with those on the margins of society, healed the sick, and forgave sinners.

By examining the life of Jesus, children learn what it is to be holy. By encountering Jesus in the sacraments and in prayer, they are motivated to live as good followers of his. Beyond that, union with Christ transforms them into him.

Grace, God's life and action in us, is the catalyst and support for becoming holy. The theological and cardinal virtues we receive at baptism strengthen us to live moral lives, and the gift of conscience guides us. When we fail to love and we sin, God's grace prompts us to feel remorse and ask forgiveness. By his mercy we have a fresh chance to live as God's children.

TEACHING MORALITY INDIRECTLY

Your classroom is like a laboratory for teaching morality, although you don't wear a white lab coat. Over and above lessons focused on commandments, virtues, and the like, you constantly impart knowledge of how to live as a Christian and form your students. For example, at a school Mass during Communion as I offered the cup to a student, the boy behind her commented, "Hey, Sharon, leave some for us!" After Mass, I met up with him and stressed how inappropriate his humor was. I asked, "Didn't you know how sacred that time is?" Sheepishly Ray answered, "I do now, Sister." That day he learned about the virtue of reverence.

You teach your students morality every time you urge them to be kind on the playground, to do their best work, not to cheat, and to obey school laws. Certain events are opportunities to teach virtues. For example, when someone visits your classroom, you teach children to be courteous, kind, and helpful. When the fire alarm sounds, you teach them to obey. You also teach your students through your example in sundry ways, such as by controlling your anger when faced with an exasperating student, by being patient with a slow learner, and by saying kind words to a student who is suffering. Modeling Christian behavior for your class makes a lasting impression.

The next sections offer suggestions for teaching aspects of moral formation.

MAKING MORAL CHOICES

In making a moral decision, we need to reflect on the consequences of each option, in particular how it will affect us, others, and our relationship with God. We also must take into consideration the commandments and church teachings.

An effective way to teach students to make good moral choices is to pose problems and have them decide what to do. For example, you find a twenty-dollar bill in the school hall; what do you do? Or at recess your friends start teasing a younger child in a mean way; what do you do? The students might role play such situations. Older students could write skits that illustrate a good moral choice.

CONSCIENCE

Conscience is defined as the voice of God speaking in us. It is actually our reason judging whether an act is good or bad. Teach your children that we are always to act according to our conscience. But point out too that we are responsible for forming our conscience by being aware of church teachings.

Here is an image that illustrates how conscience works: Conscience is like a triangle in our heart. When we disobey it, the triangle spins and its points hurt our heart. Repeatedly disobeying our conscience wears down the points. Then when the triangle spins, it no longer bothers us.

VIRTUES

White goes well with almost every color. Virtuous people survive no matter what circumstances form the backdrop of their life. A virtue is a good habit. The word *virtue* is from the Latin for "man." A person who has virtues is fully alive—as God intended us to be. St. Irenaeus once stated that the glory of God is a human being who is fully alive. Those who show extraordinary virtue we call heroes and saints. Even fictional superheroes like Superman, Batman, and Spider-Man are admired for their virtues. All virtues are ways of keeping the great commandments—loving God, self, and others.

As with all habits, virtues grow by being exercised, like muscles. Some virtues are ingrained; others we need to develop through deliberate acts and perseverance. An adage expresses the growth and goal of virtues: "Sow a thought, reap an action; sow an action, reap a habit; sow a habit, reap a character; sow a character, reap a destiny."

Key virtues are infused in us in baptism. There are the three theological virtues that relate to God and prepare us for union with him: faith, hope, and charity. They give life to all other virtues and are symbolized by a cross, anchor, and heart respectively. You might teach the Acts of Faith, Hope, and Charity. There are also the four cardinal virtues: prudence, justice, fortitude, and temperance. They are called hinge virtues because all other virtues are included in them.

Seven virtues are called capital virtues. They are humility, liberality, brotherly love, meekness, chastity, temperance, and diligence. These virtues are directly opposed to the capital vices known as the seven deadly sins: pride, avarice, envy, wrath, lust, gluttony, and sloth. Talking about the vices helps children understand the virtues. Discuss bad consequences of vices, how they hurt self or others. For example, sloth could lead to cheating on a test instead of studying; and gluttony could lead to overeating and getting sick.

TEACHING ABOUT VIRTUES

Students should be able to identify virtues and recognize how they are practiced. Here are some activities that accomplish these goals.

- Teach what virtues are in general and then define individual ones. For each virtue offer examples of how it is manifested or ask the students for them.

- Stories are a powerful way to teach, as both Jesus and Aesop knew. Read and discuss stories to teach virtue. William Bennett's *The Book of Virtues* (Simon & Schuster, 1996) is a wonderful resource for such stories. A website for plans and worksheets based on this book can be found at www.shiveracademy.com/*book-of-virtues*.html.

- Have the children role play situations that require the exercise of a virtue, such as when Mom calls them in for dinner or when a classmate is being bullied.

- When you are aware of a student practicing a virtue, praise him or her for it, especially in front of other students.

- Challenge your students to create and put on a skit illustrating a virtue. They might present it to another class or film it and post it on YouTube.

- Have the students choose a virtue and write a poem or story about it or a commercial promoting it.

- Do as one school did: devote an issue of a school newsletter to virtues. Each class was assigned a virtue and given a page to write about it. The older classes each took one of the cardinal virtues.

- Compose and carry out a prayer service on virtues, or have the students create one.

PRESENTING MODELS

White brings out the best in other colors. Likewise, good people have a positive influence on others. I learned the power of example as a young pianist. One day a composer visited my family and played one of Chopin's preludes on my piano. Every note, every crescendo and decrescendo, and every nuance were engraved on my mind. Later, when my piano teacher assigned this piece, I played it as our visitor had—so beautifully that my teacher said, "Kathleen, ask your parents if they would send you to the Cleveland Institute of Music for lessons." (Unfortunately, during the next lesson I played my usual way, and my teacher didn't even mention the Cleveland Institute of Music!)

- Let Jesus help you teach about virtues. Read aloud his words on mercy, compassion, generosity, humility, reverence, and perseverance in prayer. As gospel stories about Jesus are read, point out the virtue or virtues he practiced in them. Prepare a worksheet based on the virtues Jesus taught, perhaps a Scripture search where your students look up references and decide what virtue Jesus is teaching.

- As you teach Bible stories, have the children point out people's virtues—for example, Abraham's faith, David's courage, and Job's patience. On the other hand, discuss the virtues biblical characters failed to practice, such as the obedience Jonah lacked and the reverence for God the Israelites failed to show in worshipping the golden calf.

- In discussing the lives of Mary and the other saints, highlight their virtues. Let the children act out the scenes in the saints' lives in which a virtue is being practiced, for example, St. Martin sharing his cloak with a beggar.

- If you teach secular subjects in a Catholic school, you might discuss the virtues and vices of characters encountered in reading or English lessons or the virtues of persons studied in history class, such as courage, loyalty, and honesty.

- Call attention to people performing acts of virtue reported in the news. Invite students to bring to class newspaper articles about such people.

- A priest I know says that he was inspired to become a priest by seeing his father rise early every day to attend Mass before going to work. Ask your students what virtue their mom or dad especially practices. Then have them write letters thanking their parents for teaching them this virtue.

- Have the students write a character sketch of someone they know, focusing on a particular virtue the person exhibits.

DEVELOPING VIRTUES

At age twenty, Benjamin Franklin decided to live free from any fault. To develop his character, he chose thirteen virtues and focused on one each week. He tracked his progress on a chart. You might adapt Franklin's practice and have your class choose a few virtues and chart their daily practice of them. However, there are other ways to nurture virtues.

- Draw and cut out a tree, trunk and limbs only, and place it on a bulletin board or a wall. Draw and cut out leaves. When a student notices another student practicing a virtue, he or she prints the child's name on a leaf and adds it to the tree.
- Undertake a class project that calls for virtues, such as a drive to raise money for a good cause. Discuss the virtues involved, such as responsibility and generosity.
- Post quotations about virtues and talk about them.
- Have the children create greeting cards, posters, or little display cards with quotations about a virtue.
- At my church the children write good deeds and put them in the collection baskets during Sunday Masses. A few of these are published in each weekly bulletin. Consider introducing that practice in your parish.
- Send a handout to parents suggesting ways they could foster Christian virtues in their children.
- Focus on a virtue a week as a school or a class. Give an award to students observed practicing that virtue.

Possible virtues are religion, respect, responsibility, reverence, caring, love, compassion, patience, gentleness, self-control, generosity, peacefulness, courage, helpfulness, perseverance, courtesy, honesty, truthfulness, thankfulness, humility, reliability, pursuit of excellence, joyfulness, self-discipline, faithfulness, justice, forgiveness, kindness, friendliness, loyalty, obedience, and prudence.

A FEW WORDS ABOUT SIN

The Hebrew word for sin means "missing the mark." When we fail to love, we fall short of being who God made us to be. The original sin left us human beings weak and prone to sin. The world, the devil, and ourselves are sources of temptation. We ought to avoid people, places, and things that cause temptation. Make sure that your children know that temptations and accidents are not sins.

Teach the kinds of sins: mortal sin (serious or "deadly"), venial sin (lesser sin), and social sin (unjust structures in society against the common good that result from an accumulation of personal sins). Explain that factors like knowledge, circumstances, and freedom affect the seriousness of sin. Stress that grace helps us resist sin and that God is always ready to forgive.

Above all, encourage your students to avoid sin not because they fear punishment but because it offends the God who loves them. A white flag signals surrender. Surrendering to God and his laws makes us victors.

A FINAL TIP

The *Catechism of the Catholic Church* has four parts. The third part, "Life in Christ," is devoted to moral formation. In it is a thorough explanation of everything pertaining to morality. The section you will probably find most helpful is the one in which each of the Ten Commandments and Beatitudes is presented.

For Reflection and Discussion

- How did you learn to be good: to be just, kind, honest, obedient, and so forth?

- What people known by the children could you present as role models for them?

- What virtue in particular do your students need to cultivate? How could you help them develop it?

- How could you teach virtues indirectly?

- What social sins are prevalent today? What are their causes?

Task Four: Prayer, Our Lifeline

The color green stands for life and therefore is an appropriate color to represent prayer. Just as breathing is essential to our physical life, prayer is necessary for our spiritual life. It deepens our relationship with God. In the words of the mystic Julian of Norwich, "Prayer oneth the soul to God." If we have a five-pound teacher manual and feel pressured to cover all the content, we may be tempted to omit prayer from our lessons. That would be a mistake. Consider this: praying during your lesson might be the only time some students pray.

The church possesses a rich treasury of prayers and forms of prayer. It is a catechist's vital task to teach what it means to pray and how to pray. Our preferences for prayer change during life. By explaining various methods of praying, you equip your students with the knowledge to pray a different way when they are older. Share with them the guiding principle that we are to pray as we can, not as we can't.

Create a prayerful atmosphere as you teach. Remind the students that Jesus said that when two or three are gathered in his name, he is in their midst. He is present in your classroom ready to listen and to speak.

INTRODUCING PRAYER

Teach the traditional definition of prayer, "the raising of the mind and heart to God." But also teach St. Teresa of Avila's definition: "Prayer is conversation with one who you know loves you." You might collect definitions, present them to your children and ask which one they like best. A favorite of mine is, "Prayer is resting our head on the heart of God."

Explain that developing a relationship with God follows the pattern of developing a love relationship with a human being. We encounter each other, converse, eventually become content simply to be in the other's presence, and then ultimately enjoy union.

Share with your students that a good reason to pray is that God wants us to. Send them to the Bible to read passages that show how Jesus prayed and what he said about prayer. He gave us the Our Father, the model for all prayer. Point out that Jesus urges us to pray when he says, "Ask and you will receive; seek and you will find; knock and the door will be opened to you" (Luke 11:9). Even the initials of the words *ask, seek,* and *knock* spell *ask!*

To begin a lesson on prayer, you might have the children form groups and discuss questions such as when, where, and how they pray, and what was the first prayer they learned. As a member of your classroom community, share your answers to these questions too.

As an assignment, have your students interview people to find out their favorite way of praying. Allow time for the interviewers to share what they discovered. All will benefit from this, including you!

For one lesson on prayer, I cut out comic strips that dealt

with prayer from newspapers and magazines. It was surprising how many there were. I backed the comic strips with stiff paper and laminated them. Then I determined where they fit with my lesson. I marked each card and its matching lesson part with a letter of the alphabet. Before class I handed students a card. As I taught, when I came to a concept with a matching comic strip, I called its letter, and the student with that card read the comic strip. No one slept during that class.

Green is a symbol of springtime and rebirth. The prayer life of some students might be stifled because of misconceptions about prayer. Awaken it by dispelling these notions:

- ***Prayer must be long.*** An expert on prayer said, "A short prayer pierces the heaven." He pointed out that when a house is on fire, it's enough to call, "Fire!"

- ***It must result in many good thoughts.*** After a date, no one says, "Look at all the ideas he (or she) gave me."

- ***It must be formal.*** Words like *thee* and *thou* are not required. St. Teresa of Avila taught that we should not be bashful when addressing such a good Lord.

Prayer takes different forms. Traditionally the acronym ACTS has been used to remember them: Adoration, Contrition, Thanksgiving, and Supplication. Instead, I prefer PACT where *P* stands for Petition, because the word is linked to covenant, or agreement (and is easier for children). There are also several kinds of prayer: vocal and mental, formula prayers and spontaneous, prayers composed by others and personal prayer, and also liturgical prayer, which has been addressed in Chapter 3. A catechist's task is to offer students a whole smorgasbord of prayer methods.

PROBLEMS WITH PRAYERS

Distractions are common during prayer. They are like mosquitoes. A story tells about a man who was promised a horse if he could get through the Our Father without a distraction. In the middle of the prayer, he asked, "Do I get the saddle too?" Explain to your children that sometimes distractions are a blessing and can be worked into our prayer. For example, if a thought about our mother drifts into our mind, we might pray for her.

As we pray, sleepiness can overtake us. God loves us even while we sleep, just as a father loves the child who falls asleep in his arms.

We can be frustrated when it seems as though our prayers of petition aren't answered. Assure your children that silence from God doesn't mean that he doesn't like us! God may be answering no, not yet, or I've got a better idea. A striking example is the story of the boy who prayed to have the gift his uncle had. Every night his uncle was able to take his teeth out and place them in a glass of water. When the boy grew up, he was glad God hadn't answered his prayer. Point out that we should not aim to change God's mind but to understand it.

Mention to your children that most people probably pray more and better than they think.

TIMES OF PRAYER

Teach that any time is a good time to pray, but especially when first waking up (the Morning Offering) and right before going to bed (an Act of Contrition). Catholics also pray grace before and after meals. Encourage your children to form the habit of praying aspirations, one- or two-line prayers, throughout the day, such as "My God, I love you" and "My Jesus, mercy." Praying these prayers when we are kept waiting makes those minutes useful instead of wasted. It also keeps us aware of God, who is always aware of us.

AN ATMOSPHERE FOR CLASS PRAYER

To set the tone for class prayer, light a candle, burn incense, or play soft music. Little children might have a prayer mat to sit on during times of prayer. This could be made out of two wallpaper samples stitched together with yarn and stuffed with newspaper. Older students could draw a favorite scene and place it before them during prayer.

A calming prelude to prayer is having children set up a prayer table while music is played. On it they might place a lovely cloth, a Bible, candles, a crucifix, and religious images.

Teach the importance of silence. Tell the story of God speaking to Elijah not in wind, earthquake, or fire but in silence (1 Kings 19:11–13). Write the letters for *silent* on six cards and number the backs according to the letters in the word *listen*. Give the cards to students and have them stand in a row, facing the class and holding up their cards. Then ask them to rearrange themselves in the order of the numbers. Before praying, direct the children to have listening hands and listening feet.

FORMULA PRAYERS

Young children memorize the traditional prayers, namely, the Our Father, Hail Mary, Glory Be, the Apostles' Creed, and an Act of Contrition. Knowing these prayers enables them to pray without a book and to pray together with other Catholics. It is important to explain the meaning of a prayer's words before the children memorize them.

Here are ways to help children learn prayers by heart:

- Print name badges with the words "I know the Our Father" or whatever prayer is being learned. When children master that prayer, award them with a badge.

- Invite parents or other parishioners to be prayer listeners. Give them a chart with the children's names in a column and names of prayers as headings. Children receive a checkmark when they can recite a prayer without stumbling.

- See page 16, where suggestions for memorizing Scripture are given. These also apply to memorizing prayers.

PRAYERS OF OTHER PEOPLE

Vary the prayers you pray with the children. Introduce them to favorites, like the "Prayer of St. Francis" and Blessed Charles de Foucauld's "Prayer of Abandonment." Have a prayer pocket or a box filled with prayers contributed by you and the children, and pray one in each class. Instruct your students to make personal prayer books in which they collect prayers and compose their own.

MEDITATION

Praying is not only speaking to God, but thinking about God and listening to him. Use books like *In My Heart Room* by Mary Terese Donze, ASC, to teach children to meditate. She leads them from reflecting on an object to talking about it with Jesus present in their hearts.

Guide children through a meditation on a gospel story: Read the story. Read it again, filling in details like the setting, what people looked like, and so forth. Ask questions, linking the story to the students' lives. Allow time for silent reflection. Conclude by inviting the children to say a prayer or make a resolution.

Introduce your students to St. Ignatius' prayer with the senses. Read a story like the cure of Bartimaeus and then retell it incorporating sensory experiences. Describe what is seen and heard and what things feel, smell, and taste like. The children might imagine that they are one of the persons in a gospel story.

LECTIO DIVINA (SACRED READING)

Recent popes have stressed the value of *lectio divina,* a method of prayer that is becoming more popular. Its final goal is contemplation, the highest form of prayer. Lead your children through its four steps, which are compared to Jacob's ladder that stretched from earth to heaven:

- Read a Scripture passage being attuned to a word or phrase that catches your attention.

- Reflect on that word or phrase until you realize what God is saying to you through it.

- Respond with a prayer expressing praise, thanks, contrition, petition, or love.

- Be quiet and rest, aware of God present and loving you.

Some people add a fifth step: action.

This prayer can be conducted in small groups. In that case, children could be invited to share the word or phrase that attracted them, and to tell why.

CENTERING PRAYER

The purpose of this prayer is to center ourselves on God dwelling within us. It involves choosing a word or phrase that will act as a hook to call us back to God when our mind wanders. Simply sit quietly and focus on God. Whenever distractions occur, say the hook word.

MANTRAS

A mantra is a short prayer that is repeated over and over. It can be a Scripture verse, a line from a prayer, or a personal prayer like "I love you." The Jesus prayer ("Jesus, Son of David, have mercy on me, a sinner") is perhaps the oldest Christian mantra. When your children are too tired, sick, or worried to pray any other way, they might find comfort in praying a mantra. Even the youngest child can learn to repeat the name of Jesus as prayer.

WRITTEN PRAYERS

- ***Letters.*** Have your students write Jesus a letter and then write one from Jesus to them. Emphasize that they are not to force words when they write the letter from Jesus but rather to let the words flow from their pens or pencils. This is a powerful way to pray.

- ***Paraphrasing.*** Choose appropriate verses from a psalm and direct the children to paraphrase it. Older students might paraphrase the *Magnificat*.

- ***Original Prayer.*** List names for Jesus and have the children write a prayer addressing him under a title of their choosing.

JOURNALING

Teach older students the value of journaling as prayer and a springboard to prayer. In notebooks, they record their thoughts, collect quotations, and write prayers. You might provide questions to answer and sentences to complete, such as "My happiest moment was..." or "If I had a million dollars, I would..."

REFLECTIONS

Introduce your children to thought-provoking poems and reflections—such as "Footprints" and "A Solitary Life"—as catalysts for prayer.

THE LABYRINTH

A prayer labyrinth is a circular path that leads to a center, which stands for God's presence. It differs from a maze because there is only one path to follow. People walked labyrinths in Europe's cathedrals as a substitute for making a pilgrimage to the Holy Land. Any kind of prayer is prayed on the path. On reaching the center, people stop and reflect on God. Then they walk out of the labyrinth as though taking God with them into the world. Your students might pray on a labyrinth on grounds near you, a borrowed canvas labyrinth, or one on the Internet. If you duplicate a labyrinth on paper, the children could "walk" the path with their finger.

DEVOTIONS

The Rosary. Teach your children how and why to pray the Rosary. This beloved Catholic prayer originated when illiterate people could not pray the one hundred fifty psalms. At first they prayed one hundred fifty Our Fathers on beads. After the Hail Mary was composed, they substituted it. While the prayers are prayed, mysteries in the life of Jesus and Mary are pondered, making the Rosary the gospel on beads. After September 2001, Saint John Paul II requested that we pray the Rosary for peace. So did Mary herself when she appeared at Fatima, Portugal.

You might hold a living rosary for which people representing beads form a circle in church or outside. After participants lead their prayer at the microphone, they may place a flower or vigil light in front of a statue of Mary.

Your students might enjoy making rosaries, perhaps by using kits from companies. One school held a contest in which families competed to make the most unique rosary. The winning rosary was made of corks and washers.

The Stations of the Cross. The stations, or way of the cross, came about as a substitute for a pilgrimage to the Holy Land, where Jesus suffered and died. We most often pray the fourteen stations during Lent. Your students might write their own reflections or a poem for each station. Sometimes children at a Catholic school or a parish school of religion (catechetical program) lead the entire school in praying the stations by forming a tableau (living picture) for each one.

Divine Mercy Devotion. This comparatively new devotion stems from a vision of Jesus that St. Faustina Kowalski, a Polish nun, had in 1931. She saw Jesus touching his heart from which two rays came forth, which stood for the blood and water that streamed from his pierced heart. Jesus instructed Faustina to have an image like this made, along with the words "Jesus, I trust in you." In 2000, St. John Paul II declared the Second Sunday of Easter "Divine Mercy Sunday." You might teach your students to pray the Chaplet of Divine Mercy.

SPONTANEOUS PRAYER

Even adults get tongue-tied when asked for spontaneous prayer. You might allow your children to write their "spontaneous" prayers first before they pray them aloud.

SOME PRAYER ACTIVITIES

- Let students take turns leading the class in a prayer of their choice.

- Use a slide or poster to prompt a prayer.

- Hold round-robin prayer: Each child contributes a sentence or a word.

- Popcorn prayer: Students spontaneously add a sentence or word to a prayer.

- Alphabet prayer: For each letter, students name something for which to praise and thank God.

- Hold a retreat day with a theme. Holy Week would be an appropriate time for this.

- Prayer services. Conclude a unit with a prayer service to let religious mysteries sink into the children's hearts. Include a hymn, a Scripture reading, a litany, time for reflection, and a prayer.

WEBSITES FOR PRAYER

www.sacredspace.ie
(a popular Jesuit site offering prayer for every day)

www.usccb.org *(Click on "prayer and worship.")*

www.ewtn.com/devotionals/prayer_saint.asp *(many prayers)*

www.prayingeachday.org *(a daily prayer)*

The Divine Office (Prayer of Christians):
www.ebreviary.com *(prayers of the day)*

The Rosary: www.comepraytherosary.org

Labyrinths: www.lessons4living.com/finger_labyrinth.htm

Stations of the Cross:
www.catholic.org/clife/prayers/station.php?id=1

Stations for children:
www.cptryon.org/prayer/child/stations/index.html

Tell your children that we know we are praying well if we are doing God's will. Point out that one thing we can pray for is to have the gift of prayer. Green is a sign of growth. With God's help, through prayer our children's relationship with Jesus will grow and deepen.

For Reflection and Discussion

- How would you define prayer?
- What is your favorite way to pray? Has this changed as you've aged? If so, how?
- What is your favorite prayer?
- What personal experiences of prayer could you share with your students?
- What form of prayer might you teach your students to expand their repertoire of prayer?

Task Five: Community, A Union *of* Love

Yellow, the color of the sun, sunflowers, and gold, is a bright, happy color, ideal for representing community, which is a source of joy. A community is a group of people who are united because they share common values. In a recent homily, a priest from New York told of how one day for breakfast the rectory housekeeper from the south prepared grits, a dish unfamiliar to him. When he asked for just one grit, the housekeeper and other priests roared with laughter. Like grits, a community comes packaged together.

God is a Trinity, a community of three divine Persons bonded together by love. Our creator made us social beings too. We require the comradeship, support, and thoughts of others to thrive and live well. That is why solitary confinement is a severe punishment. Relationships are a precious characteristic of being human. Teaching about community and how to build it is of prime importance today when our world is marked by strife due to multiple divisions between people, nations, races, and religions. What a difference it would make if everyone followed the golden rule: Do to others as you would have them do to you.

GOD'S COMMUNITIES

When God first revealed himself, he called the Israelites not as individuals but as a people, a community. They were God's chosen people, bonded together by a sacred covenant with him. He also saved, taught, and punished the Israelites as a group.

To Jesus, community was a priority. He called the Twelve, and for perhaps three years they traveled together, sharing food and finances. He sent his disciples out not singly but two by two. Jesus taught how to foster community: be humble, be as simple as a child, forgive without limit, and above all, love one another as you love yourself.

The first Christians were "of one heart and soul" (Acts 4:32). They were such a tight-knit community that they "had all things in common; they would sell their possessions and goods and distribute the proceeds to all, as any had need... they spent much time together in the temple" (Acts 2:44–46). These early followers of Jesus were united by love for him and one another.

The church is a community so completely bonded that it is known as a body, the body of Christ. Members count on one another for assistance and support in times of need, doubt, or crisis.

Another name for the church is the communion of saints. It comprises people of faith in heaven, in purgatory, and on earth, or, as someone quipped, all saints, all souls, and all sorts. A task of catechesis is to teach what it means to be part of this grand community and how to be a responsible member.

THE CLASSROOM COMMUNITY

You and your students are a subset of the church. You form a Christian community, that is, a group of people who are journeying through life together sharing belief in Jesus Christ, growing in faith, and celebrating it. Communicate to your class the concept that you are united in Christ and trying to deepen your relationship with him together. As a catechist, you are not the sage on the stage, but a guide at the side. You and your students learn from one another.

Provide opportunities for sharing faith. This can be done in whole class discussions or more intimately by having the students discuss in groups topics such as prayer, being a disciple, and who Jesus is for them. The children might form their own groups, but here are ways to guarantee a good mix:

- Decide how many students you would like in a group. (Five is considered ideal.) Divide your class total by that number and have the students count off up to the quotient. Call those with the same number to form a group.

- Pull as many cards from a deck as you have students, insuring that you have about equal numbers of each suit. Have the children choose a card and form groups according to suits.

- Direct the class to line up and then pair off the students from both ends of the line.

- Label index cards with colors (or animals or anything else) and have each child pick one. Then call all the blues together and so on.

Be creative in determining group leaders. They could be the children whose birthday is next, whose name has the most letters, who live the farthest away or who are the tallest, the shortest, the oldest, or the youngest.

Your class is a segment of the school community. Work with other teachers to plan activities that allow all of the school children to interact, such as a school play, a program, or a special prayer service. Or have your children do something for another class. For example, they might write letters to the first communicants, put on a skit for a younger class, or make cards for those graduating from a Catholic school or catechetical program.

THE FAMILIES OF YOUR CHILDREN

The members of the church community closest to your children are their parents and siblings. It is within their families that your children first hear the Good News of Jesus, pray, and learn how to live as Jesus taught. Make every effort to engage family members in activities with your students and with other families. Hold family nights, invite parents to be guest speakers in your class, and assign homework and projects for families to carry out together. While children are in class, arrange for parents (and grandparents) to meet for Bible study, a presentation, or just socializing.

One way to create a sense of community among families is to schedule a day or week when everyone will pray for one of the families. You might also keep families apprised of what other children and families are doing through newsletters or emails. Invite families to participate in class or school Masses. After all, the Eucharist is the source and summit of the church community. An open house day during which parents sit in on classes is another option. Families meet one another, and parents might even learn something about the faith that they didn't know.

THE PARISH

Help your children realize that they are part of the parish community. Foster a relationship between them and their priest(s) and deacon(s) by inviting these ordained men to teach a lesson or part of a lesson. Introduce the children to other parish leaders, perhaps by holding a panel in which each one explains how they serve the parish. Or have children interview them and report to the class.

Older students might create a booklet or a PowerPoint presentation about their parish and its activities. To help with that project, provide the class with a set of church bulletins, or direct the students to your parish website.

The children might become prayer partners to senior parishioners and enjoy at least one special activity with them, such as a luncheon. Your children might write to the RCIA catechumens and candidates, welcoming them into the church. Encourage parents to participate in parish functions—Christmas concerts, parish picnics or festivals, parish missions, service projects, and the like—as a family.

Students can be taught to be active, responsible members of the parish family. For example, suggest that they become altar servers, hosts at receptions and fish fries, and cooks when baked goods are needed. They might contribute their own money to the collection basket each week!

Hold programs where the Catholic school children and those who attend the parish school of religion participate together, such as a vacation Bible school or a Lenten retreat.

THE DIOCESE AND BEYOND

Alert parents to opportunities for the children to take part in diocesan activities. For example, each summer the Cleveland Diocese holds a FEST for families, with booths, Christian bands, a raffle, games, an evening Mass, and fireworks. Being gathered with tens of thousands of other Catholics makes the children aware of the larger church community and strengthens their connection to it. A visit to your diocesan cathedral is another way to imbue your children with a sense of belonging to the wider church.

Keep your children informed about news in the universal church. Gather information from Catholic newspapers and magazines as well as from websites like zenit.com, which provides daily e-mails with the pope's homilies and activities and church events throughout the world.

CARING FOR THE COMMUNITY

As a warm, friendly color, yellow represents the attitudes we should have toward one another. A beautiful story that illustrates community is about children in a race. As they sprinted, one boy who was overweight and awkward lagged far behind. Another child noticed this. He stopped and began jogging backwards. Other children joined him until all of the racers were running back to the boy bringing up the rear. Two of them linked arms with him, and then as a whole, the children ran toward the finish line. Together they broke the ribbon and all cried, "We won! We won!"

Instill in your children kindness and respect for other members of the community. Romans 12:10–21 is a recipe for kindness. Ask your children for examples of how they could follow the advice in this passage. Teach that being polite and using courteous words show respect for others. An acronym for avoiding harmful words is the word *think*. The words of a Christian should be *T*rue, *H*elpful, *I*nspiring, *N*ecessary, and *K*ind.

Have your children role play or make posters showing children being kind and respectful, for instance, by receiving a punishment well, cleaning their room, coming on time, paying attention when someone is talking, not disturbing an animal that is sleeping or eating, having manners, respecting privacy, picking up a fallen object, paying a compliment, writing a note, and helping a neighbor with yard work.

The United States bishops have stated seven principles that undergird just relations. This is nothing new. Ages ago, when I was an eighth grader, a long-range assignment was to make a booklet with a page on each Christian social principle. This is the present form of the Catholic social themes to be integrated into catechesis:

- Life and dignity of the human person
- Call to family, community, and the pursuit of the common good
- Rights and responsibilities
- Option for the poor and vulnerable
- Dignity of work and the rights of workers
- Solidarity
- Care for God's creation

SERVING OTHERS

Albert Schweitzer once said to students from the United States, "I do not know what your destiny will be, but one thing I know; the only ones among you who will really be happy are those who have sought and found how to serve." Similarly, psychiatrist Karl Menninger advised that to shake off depression, cross the railroad tracks and help someone on the other side.

Service projects are an integral part of preparation for the sacrament of confirmation for good reason. Jesus urged his followers to serve, and he demonstrated by giving us a poignant example. On the night before he died, Jesus washed the apostles' feet, the task of a servant. Jesus also taught that those who feed the hungry, give drink to the thirsty, clothe the naked, welcome the stranger, and visit the sick and imprisoned will merit a place in his kingdom. Jesus regards caring for the least members in God's family as caring for him. This is motivation enough to teach the spiritual and corporal works of mercy.

- Pope Francis has captured the world's attention and admiration because, by words and deeds, he frequently teaches us to serve. Refer to him as a model and quote some of his teachings on serving others.

- Assign reports on people known for serving the needy and oppressed, including those engaged in social service today in your country or city. Models from the past are Vincent de Paul, Dorothy Day, Martin de Porres, John Baptist de la Salle, Mother Cabrini, Mother Teresa of Calcutta, Damian of Molokai, Oscar Romero, Martin Luther King, Jr., Mahatma Gandhi, and Florence Nightingale.

- Explore ways that your children can become involved in projects that aid the needy. Maybe they can assist at a soup kitchen, visit a nursing home, prepare packages for the missions, or raise funds for Habitat for Humanity.

- Keep updated on parish service projects, and invite the children to participate if possible.

CARING FOR CREATION

All things on heaven and earth were created by God and redeemed by Jesus. They reflect God's goodness and glory. God entrusted creation to us. When we are good stewards, we are co-creators. Teach your children that the gifts of creation are intended to be shared by all people, including future members of the community. St. Francis of Assisi is the patron of ecology. His "Canticle of the Creatures," in which we call on created things to praise God, is a fitting introduction to the concept of stewardship.

Scripture verses that can be incorporated into lessons or prayer services about creation are Genesis 1; Psalm 8; Psalm 104; Job 38, 39; and Daniel 3:57–81.

Let the children talk about things they are responsible for and how they take care of them, such as toys, clothes, a pet, house, school supplies, and their computer.

Acquaint your children with the 4 Rs—ways to save the earth: reduce, reuse, recycle, and repair. Ask for examples of how they can carry these out, for example, by not leaving water running, turning off lights, and avoiding Styrofoam containers. Have them make posters encouraging an aspect of the 4 Rs.

Involve your students in recycling projects. They might begin one at the school or parish.

Engage your children in programs geared to protecting our natural resources like clean water and forests. Educate them about sustainable programs and involve them in organizations that protect the environment and animals headed for extinction. Keep them informed about environmental issues.

Share stories and anecdotes with the theme of caring for creation, such as the starfish story. This is one variation adapted from *The Star Thrower* by Loren Eiseley. One day after a storm, a beach was covered with starfish. A man walking along saw a young girl pick up starfish and gently toss them into the ocean. "Miss," he asked, "why are you throwing starfish into the ocean?"

"The sun is up, and the tide is going out. They need water. If I do not throw them in, they will die."

"But there are miles and miles of starfish. You can't possibly make a difference."

Throwing another starfish into the ocean, the girl replied, "It made a difference for that one."

One school held a retreat day with the theme of caring for creation. Every twelve minutes, each class traveled to a different room for an interactive session on one of these topics: body, earth, water, air, soul, animals, trees, consumerism, and the value of buying locally. In the earth session, children learned about compost. For the soul session, the pastor led them in a meditation on God's life. The day included making an individual globe as well as placing a thumbprint on an enormous globe to be displayed in the school hall. The culmination was a prayer service on creation. Parish schools of religion can easily adapt this memorable activity.

OUR HEAVENLY MEMBERS

The yellow of smiley faces is a cheerful color. St. Teresa of Avila stated that a sad saint is a sorry saint. Saints are happy people. We can be happy because in the communion of saints we enjoy a relationship with the saints, our friends in high places. The preface for a Mass for Holy Men and Women states that through the saints God gives us an example, friendship, and strength and protection by their prayer. They spur us on to victory—everlasting glory.

Preeminent among the saints is Mary, the Mother of God. Besides teaching the doctrines about the Blessed Virgin, make sure the children understand that she is not a goddess but a flesh and blood human being. Moreover, Mary is their heavenly mother who loves them and intercedes for them. Teach your children what we know about Mary from Scripture, her virtues, titles, prayers and devotions to her, and her appearances on earth.

Introducing your children to the saints inspires them to be holy. As a friend from Kenya remarked: "No one stands by the fire without being warmed." When the feast day of a saint comes along, take a few minutes to talk about him or her. Begin class with a prayer written by a saint or a prayer to a saint. Incorporate quotations from saints in your lessons. In your parish bulletin or family newsletters request medals, pictures, and holy cards of the saints that you can award as prizes. Choose a class patron saint and suggest to families that they choose a patron saint.

These activities can familiarize your students with the saints:

- Have the children prepare unique reports on their patron saint or a favorite saint by means of puppets, a skit, an interview with the saint, or a PowerPoint presentation.

- Make a class mural of a saint's life.

- Invite speakers to talk about their favorite saint.

- Conduct a contest in which families compete to see who can identify the saints described or pictured on a worksheet.

- For the feast of All Saints, have the students dress as their favorite saint. They might process into church for Mass that day.

- Play games like saint bingo or a "saint bee" with "Who am I?" riddles.

- Create worksheets about saints, such as a word search or a crossword puzzle.

- Have the children design banners, posters, book jackets, scrapbooks, or websites about the saints.

- Direct the children to write poems, newspaper articles, or obituaries for the saints.

LIFESTYLES

All members of the community are called to be holy. They will win their yellow halo by following the particular vocation or lifestyle to which they are also called. It is as though we are all on a highway to heaven but traveling in different lanes. Introduce your students to all lifestyles: the ordained, married, consecrated religious, and single.

You might invite representatives from each vocation to form a panel and talk about their lifestyle. If possible, visit a local convent or seminary. Contact your diocesan vocation office for opportunities for your students to explore their options. Teach them how to discern their vocation.

ECUMENISM

Globalization, immigration, and intermarriage of people of different faiths have made us more aware of other religions. A key aspect of teaching community is preparing your children to live and work with people of other faith traditions. Inculcate in your students an attitude of respect for other believers, who are our brothers and sisters. Teach what members of other faith traditions believe, emphasizing what we have in common with them. Plant in your students' hearts a desire for Christian unity but not at the expense of compromising the truths that the Catholic Church holds. An ideal time to teach ecumenism is the Week of Prayer for Christian Unity, celebrated annually from January 18 to January 25.

Topics related to community are exciting, and what more exciting color is there than yellow?

For Reflection and Discussion

- What qualities must a person possess in order to be a community builder?
- What outstanding experience of community have you experienced?
- Celebrations are great ways to foster community. What celebration can you plan for your children or arrange for them to participate in?
- How can you make your children more aware of the saints?
- What service activities have you engaged in with your children? What service activities could you carry out?

7

Task Six: Mission *to the* World

Purple, the color of royalty and regal robes, is the perfect color for mission. The mission of every disciple is to grow the kingdom of God, bringing others to acknowledge Jesus Christ as Lord and King. Moreover, violet, which has the most powerful visible wavelength, is at the top of the rainbow spectrum, right next to the invisible ultraviolet rays. For that reason, it is associated with spirituality, a relationship with God that mission aims to establish and foster.

At the beginning of his public ministry, Jesus said to his apostles, "Come." But at the end, he said, "Go." On a mountain before ascending into heaven, Jesus charged, "Go therefore and make disciples of all nations, baptizing them in the name of the Father and of the Son and of the Holy Spirit, and teaching them to obey everything that I have commanded you" (Matthew 28:19–20). This command is known as the Great Commission. Jesus intends for us to be missionary disciples.

Delivering the Good News of salvation is called evangelizing. In Greek the prefix *eu* means good or healthy. *Angel,* the root word of evangelize, is derived from a word that means messenger, or one who announces. Loosely translated, then, evangelize means "help is on the way." With our baptism came the responsibility to be carriers of the message of salvation—in other words, to be angels!

The *Catechism of the Catholic Church* teaches: "Those who with God's help have welcomed Christ's call and freely responded to it are urged on by love of Christ to proclaim the Good News everywhere in the world" (no. 3).

Saint John Paul II, in his encyclical *Mission of the Redeemer,* reminded us, "No believer in Christ, no institution of the Church can avoid this supreme duty: to proclaim Christ to all peoples" (no. 3). This is the essential task of the church, for, as Blessed Pope Paul VI claimed in his apostolic exhortation *On Evangelization in the Modern World*, "She [the church] exists in order to evangelize" (no. 14). You might read these two documents.

Sharing the Good News is the primary way we serve people. More than ever, the world needs to hear the story of Jesus and salvation. A hedonistic, consumer-oriented mentality pervades society, sickening it. Violence is rampant in other countries and on our own streets. Many people are left yearning for meaning and hope. Whether they realize it or not, they long for a connection with the divine. Who will tell them that God is good and loving, that Jesus died and rose for love of them, that there is an afterlife, and that there are people who care about them? There is an urgent need for evangelization to bring about joy and set people free.

Someone observed that for Catholics the Great Commission is the Great Omission. Pope Francis described this neglect in terms of the parable of the shepherd who leaves the ninety-nine sheep to search for the missing one. The Holy Father said that we have the one sheep, but we have lost the other ninety-nine! He urged us to feel the fervor, the apostolic zeal to go out and find the ninety-nine instead of just combing the fleece of the one, which is an easier task. Too many Catholics assume that our church obligations are limited to paying, praying, and obeying. We must remember that we are also to relay. In fact, at the end of Mass we are sent forth to carry out this mission.

Our last three popes have launched a "new evangelization" focused on Catholics who have left the church and those who are Catholic in name only. This is in addition to reaching out to the unchurched. It's up to us to attract and train new disciples for Jesus, fervent disciples on fire for introducing others to him.

EXPLAIN OUR TASK

By the very act of teaching children about Jesus, you are evangelizing. A facet of your ministry is to pass the baton on to them and make them evangelizers too. You might assume that children are too young to carry out this mission. However, sometimes they, with their generosity and simple love, can be the best apostles and the most eager. Plus, forming in children a missionary heart today will impact the future church. Pope Francis has said, "I encourage educators to cultivate in little ones the missionary spirit, so that there may arise from among them witnesses of the tenderness of God and announcers of his love."

Purple is associated with wealth and luxury. Point out to the children that when they behold something marvelous, such as a sunset or a rainbow, they call other people's attention to it. We have a natural impulse to share good things. We are wealthy because we possess the wonderful news of salvation. We should want everyone else to know it too. Also, when we have a good friend, we enjoy introducing him or her to other people. When Jesus is our friend, and an amazing one at that, wouldn't we want everyone else to meet him?

Explain to the children that Jesus commanded us to tell others the Good News. This news is that, out of love for us, God the Father sent his Son to save us, and, by dying and rising, Jesus made it possible for us to live forever with God in his kingdom of heaven. When people know and love Jesus, they will live by his teachings and make his kingdom of peace and justice realized on earth. By emphasizing the need for Christians to evangelize, you may be planting the seed of a missionary vocation in some child.

To illustrate evangelizing, refer to models in the Bible:

- After the apostle Andrew spent time with Jesus, he told his brother Peter about him and brought Peter to meet Jesus.

- The apostle Philip introduced the apostle Nathanael to Jesus.

- A Samaritan woman who met Jesus at a well spoke about him in her city, and many Samaritans came to believe.

- As soon as Mary Magdalene encountered the risen Jesus, she went to tell the disciples that she saw him.

- After the Holy Spirit came upon the apostles, they preached to people in Jerusalem and other towns.

- On meeting the risen Jesus, Saul (Paul) became a Christian. He founded churches, made three missionary journeys in the Roman Empire, and wrote letters to teach and encourage new Christians.

Present missionary saints as models. Tell about, or have the children report on, saints like Paul, Francis Xavier, Isaac Jogues, Junipero Serra, and Frances Cabrini.

INVOLVE CHILDREN IN THE MISSION

In our mostly blue and green world, purple is rare. Purple flowers—lavender, orchid, lilac, and violet—are considered precious, as is the Good News we proclaim. Suggest ways that your students could bring others to know and love Jesus or ask them for ideas. They might read or tell friends or younger children stories about Jesus or invite them to a church service or activity. A woman told me that one day someone suggested that her family view the beautiful artwork and stained-glass windows in the shrine of the Poor Clare nuns. This visit led to the whole family becoming Catholic. Today that woman's son is a priest!

To teach the role of prayer in mission work, present St. Thérèse of Lisieux, the co-patron of the missions with St. Francis Xavier. Why does a nun who never left her cloistered convent have this title? She prayed for the missions and once prayed for the salvation of a condemned murderer. Let the children know that they too help spread the Good News by praying for the success of missionaries. They can also pray that Catholics who no longer practice the faith return to it. Inform them that St. Monica stormed heaven, praying that her wayward son, Augustine, would become a Christian. After many years, he not only embraced the faith but became a great bishop and a saint.

Make your children aware of missionary work today both in foreign countries and in their own land (home missions).

- Acquaint them with lay missionary societies and missionary religious communities, such as Maryknoll and Missionaries of Charity. Inform them too of missionary endeavors of religious congregations not specifically founded for missions. My own teaching community, for example, has missions in India, Africa, and Nicaragua.

- Present to your students the mission work going on in a particular country.
- Have the children make a report on the missions at work in a country assigned to them.
- Invite someone who works at a mission or has visited a mission to speak to your children about the work carried out there.
- Have the children explore the work of the Catholic Extension society, which supports poor mission dioceses in the United States. Its quarterly magazine can be found on the Internet.

Arrange to have your children participate in activities that support the missions sponsored by your parish or school. Some parishes adopt a partner parish in another country, visit it, and engage in various activities to support its parishioners. The children might carry out mission activities of their own. They could hold a fundraiser for a particular mission or adopt a missionary and write to him or her, offering prayers and donations.

The Missionary Childhood Association (formerly Holy Childhood Association) provides material for engaging children in missionary activity. See www.onefamilyinmission.org/hca.html. Maryknoll offers a free magazine classroom program at http://www.maryknollsociety.org/index.php/classroom-program-form. Material is also available from the Catholic Relief Services.

Acquaint your children with the World Mission Rosary designed by Archbishop Fulton J. Sheen. Each decade is a different color that calls to mind a region where the church evangelizes: green for the forests and grasslands of Africa; blue for the ocean surrounding the Pacific islands; white to symbolize Europe, where the Holy Father lives; red for the fire of faith that brought missionaries to the Americas; and yellow, like the morning light of the East, for Asia. Purchase mission rosaries and encourage your children to pray them.

Have your students write a few sentences about why they are Catholic. Then, when someone poses that question to them, they will be prepared.

If your parish has an evangelization committee, encourage the children's families to join it. Even young children can stuff envelopes and be greeters at the church door.

Inform your children that the best way to bring people to Jesus is by example. It's often said that St. Francis told his companions on entering a town, "Preach and if necessary use words." When people notice us praying grace in a restaurant, going to church, wearing ashes on Ash Wednesday, serving in a soup kitchen, and being kind, they might be prompted to investigate our faith.

Finally, point out to your children that the more they learn about God and their faith in religion class, the closer they are to Jesus through prayer and the sacraments, the more faithfully they live and love as Jesus taught, and the more united they are to the community of the church, the better evangelizers they will be.

Notice that by teaching all six tasks of catechesis, you prepare your children to be evangelizers.

For Reflection and Discussion

- Who evangelized you? How?
- How can you tap into programs offered by your diocesan mission office and office of evangelization?
- How would you answer the question "Why are you a Catholic?"
- How does your parish evangelize? What can you do to participate in its programs?
- In what ways can you use social media to evangelize?

Your Aim: A Complete Picture

Recently I put together a brand-new jigsaw puzzle. To my chagrin, one piece was missing! Not only was the lovely country scene incomplete, but I was deprived of the satisfaction that comes from snapping the final piece into place. Luckily, I had not intended to display the puzzle on the wall. The six tasks of catechesis can be compared to six interlocking pieces that complete the picture of faith formation. All are important and in fact necessary.

Another fitting analogy for the unity of the six tasks is the human body. All members—eyes, arms, feet, and so on—are unique and have their own functions, but together they form one entity. Likewise, the six dimensions of catechesis combine to make up the totality of our faith.

The *General Directory for Catechesis* shows how the tasks are intertwined by pointing out that knowledge of the faith, liturgical life, and the following of Christ are gifts of the Holy Spirit and the result of prayer. At the same time, they are a duty for those engaged in spiritual and moral study and obliged to give Christian witness (87).

EARLY CHRISTIAN FORMATION

Each catechetical task was clearly present in the faith development of the first Christians:

1. (Knowledge) Certain individuals met Jesus and heard him speak. They learned about God, the kingdom of God, and Jesus himself. They came to have faith in Jesus as the Son of God and our Savior and passed on this knowledge to others.

2. (Liturgy) The apostles participated in the Last Supper. After Jesus ascended, church leaders baptized, celebrated the Eucharist, and anointed the sick.

3. (Moral formation) The first Christians were instructed in moral standards that surpassed the laws they had been following. They were challenged by the Beatitudes and learned the importance of learning to love even one's enemies.

4. (Prayer) Jesus taught the Our Father and encouraged praying with confidence, perseverance, and humility.

5. (Community) The first Christians were a group of disciples, followers of Jesus. After Pentecost, they were a close-knit community who cared for one another and the poor.

6. (Mission) They proclaimed the Good News of salvation in the face of persecution, and some spread the faith in foreign lands.

THE PEDAGOGY OF GOD

A modern trend in catechetics is to take as a model the pedagogy of God, how God taught and formed his people. In the Old Testament, we can detect the six dimensions of catechesis in God's dealings with the Israelites.

1. (Knowledge) God imparted knowledge of himself through revelation by speaking and acting in people's lives. Abraham came to know God as the one God who does not desire human sacrifice and who would bless all nations through Abraham's descendants. Moses learned God's personal name and witnessed that God is a saving God. The prophets spoke for God and about God. Ultimately, God sent his Son as the fullest revelation of himself.

2. (Liturgy) God gave Moses specific directions for worship and the priesthood. Later God told King David that his son Solomon would build the temple, which he did.

3. (Moral formation) God gave the Israelites the laws recorded in Deuteronomy, including the Ten Commandments. In the period of the judges, God taught the Israelites not to worship idols by letting the Israelites be attacked whenever they did so. When the Israelites strayed from the law, God sent prophets to warn them.

4. (Prayer) God gave his people the hundred and fifty psalms and the canticles in the Bible. People like Abraham, Solomon, Jeremiah, and Esther served as models of prayer.

5. (Community) God saved the Israelites from slavery in Egypt and made a covenant with them as a people.

6. (Mission) God sent individuals to deliver his messages and carry out his purposes: Moses, Aaron, Gideon, Esther, and prophets like Samuel, Jonah, and John the Baptist.

COMPLEMENTARY TASKS

The six integral tasks of catechesis are closely connected in multiple ways. They are like strands of colored yarn woven together that sometimes crisscross and overlay one another.

Knowing the faith leads to celebrating the liturgy. On the other hand, the liturgy expands and deepens the faith. Knowing the faith spurs us on to conversing with God in prayer, while praying increases our faith. Knowing the faith also makes us want to live it and to celebrate it with a community of those who have the same vision. Interacting with other believers fosters our own faith. Then too, once we know the faith, we are bound to spread it as Jesus commanded. We are compelled to share it with others.

Liturgy too is related to the other tasks. As we celebrate the sacraments, we learn more about our faith. Liturgy actually is prayer. We engage in liturgy together with the Christian community, which is strengthened by it. Through the liturgy we receive grace to live a good Christian life. The liturgy sends us forth to share the Good News.

Through *prayer* we cultivate a deep relationship with God. As a result, we thirst to know more about our faith, we desire to encounter God by celebrating the liturgy, we wish to live according to God's laws, we are moved to love other people whom God loves, and we are impelled to bring others to know God.

Moral formation involves practicing the virtues of faith and religion, praying, celebrating the sacraments, promoting justice and peace among our brothers and sisters, and pointing others to a better way of life. On the other hand, these actions contribute to moral formation.

As a *community* we grow in faith, pray together, celebrate the sacraments, support one another in living as Christians, and work together to build up the community with new members.

A *mission* apostolate assumes that the faith is known. It is fueled by prayer and the sacraments. The witness of our good

Christian living makes our mission successful, as does the support of the community.

IMPLICATIONS FOR CATECHISTS

In planning your lessons for the year, make sure to teach all six tasks. A good religion series provides for this. Some lessons will be devoted to teaching the faith, some will be on moral formation, and so forth. At times, an individual lesson will include more than one task. If you are fortunate enough to have such a manual, you simply have to "paint by number" and follow the plans as they are. Otherwise, you will need to design a few of your own plans or adapt the given ones.

Suppose a lesson teaches that the Bible is God's word and that the Holy Spirit inspired the human authors. It might cover the parts of the Bible, the kinds of books, and how to interpret a Scripture citation. All of these pertain to knowledge of the faith. How improved the lesson would be if other tasks were added, for example in these ways:

- Teach the children to pray the Prayer to the Holy Spirit before reading the Bible (prayer).
- Refer to the readings from last Sunday's Mass (liturgy).
- For practice in looking up a passage, choose some that are moral instructions (moral formation).
- Form groups and ask the children to share their favorite Bible passages (community).
- Give students the assignment of telling a sibling or friend a story about Jesus (mission).

For Reflection and Discussion

- Do the lessons in your manual offer ways to fulfill all six tasks? If not, how can you adapt them?
- Choose a day in your life, maybe yesterday or today. How did learning the faith, prayer, liturgy, moral formation, community, and mission come into play?
- Think back to the days you were catechized. Were all six tasks carried out or was one or more slighted?
- How would you draw a diagram that illustrated the six tasks?
- Which task is the easiest for you to teach? The most challenging? Why?

EPILOGUE

Associating each of the six catechetical tasks with a color has rich significance because of the relationship between colors and light. Visible light is composed of colors. We observe this when light passes through a prism and separates into the colors of the spectrum—what we know as rainbow colors. In Genesis, God's first creation was light, and light, like God, is rather mysterious. Although God is pure spirit and invisible, his holiness and glory are aptly represented by the image of light.

Expressing God's essence as light is rooted in Scripture. God appeared to Moses in a burning bush and led the Israelites through the desert as a pillar of fire. In Psalm 104:2, God is "wrapped in light as with a garment." Contact with God leads to a share in his glory. That is why whenever Moses spoke with God, his face became so radiant that afterwards he had to cover it with a veil (Exodus 34:29–35).

In the New Testament, too, God is identified with light: "God is light" (1 John 1:5). The Gospel of John introduces Jesus as the light shining in the darkness (John 1:3–9), and Jesus calls himself the light of the world (John 8:12). During the Transfiguration, the face of Jesus "shone like the sun, and his clothes became dazzling white" (Matthew 17:2). In heaven, there is "no need of sun or moon to shine on it, for the glory of God is its light, and its lamp is the Lamb" (Revelation 21:23). Jesus exhorted, "Believe in the light, so that you may become children of light" (John 12:36). St. Paul reminds us that we are called to live as children of the light (Ephesians 5:8).

Just as colors blend to form light, when the six tasks are combined in your teaching, you provide light for your students. You dispel the darkness of ignorance of the faith and enable them to see. Furthermore, as you accomplish this, you assist your children on their journey to becoming more Godlike and reflecting God's glory. After walking in the light on earth, may they—and you—arrive at God's kingdom and have no need of sun or LED lights, for there the brilliant light of God shines without end.